My United States

West Virginia

MARTIN SCHWABACHER

Children's Press®
An Imprint of Scholastic Inc.

Content Consultant

James Wolfinger, PhD, Associate Dean and Professor
College of Education, DePaul University, Chicago, Illinois

Library of Congress Cataloging-in-Publication Data
Names: Schwabacher, Martin, author.
Title: West Virginia / by Martin Schwabacher.
Description: New York, NY : Children's Press, an imprint of Scholastic, 2019. | Series: A true book | Includes
   bibliographical references and index.
Identifiers: LCCN 2018000996 | ISBN 9780531235850 (library binding) | ISBN 9780531250983 (pbk.)
Subjects: LCSH: West Virginia—Juvenile literature.
Classification: LCC F241.3 .S34 2012 | DDC 975.4—dc23
LC record available at https://lccn.loc.gov/2018000996

Photographs ©: cover: Backyard Productions/Alamy Images; back cover bottom: Tim Mainiero/Shutterstock; back cover ribbon: AliceLiddelle/Getty Images; 3 bottom: Wiskerke/Alamy Images; 3 map: Jim McMahon/Mapman ®; 4 left: MR.Silaphop Pongsai/Shutterstock; 4 right: Isselee/Dreamstime; 5 top: Harrison Shull/Aurora Photos; 5 bottom: WENN .com 6/24/2016/age fotostock; 6 bottom: ablokhin/iStockphoto; 7 center: Pat & Chuck Blackley/Alamy Images; 7 top: Avmedved/Dreamstime; 7 bottom: Lawrence Weslowski Jr/Dreamstime; 8-9: Jon Bilous/Dreamstime; 11: Kenneth Keifer/iStockphoto; 12: Skip Brown/Getty Images; 13: Skip Brown/Getty Images; 14: Larry Keller, Lititz Pa./Getty Images; 15: Ruaridh Connellan/BarcroftImages/Barcroft Media/Getty Images; 16-17: DenisTangneyJr/iStockphoto; 19: Andrew Lichtenstein/Corbis/Getty Images; 20: Tigatelu/Dreamstime; 22 left: Alancotton/Dreamstime; 22 right: Brothers Good/Shutterstock; 23 bottom right: MR.Silaphop Pongsai/Shutterstock; 23 center left: Le Do/Shutterstock; 23 center right: Mohammed Anwarul Kabir Choudhury/Dreamstime; 23 bottom left: MCDinosaurhunter/Wikimedia; 23 top right: Isselee/Dreamstime; 24-25: Carol M. Highsmith/Library of Congress; 27: ND/Roger Viollet/Getty Images; 29: MPI/Getty Images; 30 right: MPI/StringerGetty Images; 30 left: Carol M. Highsmith/Library of Congress; 31 top right: The West Virginia Mine Wars Museum/Kenneth King Collection; 31 top left: Alancotton/Dreamstime; 31 bottom: Lewis Wickes Hine/Library of Congress; 32: Lewis Wickes Hine/Library of Congress; 33: Bain News Service/Library of Congress; 34-35: Billy E. Barnes/PhotoEdit; 36: Aspenphoto/Dreamstime; 37: Mark Wilson/Getty Images; 38: Jim West/Alamy Images; 39: Jim West/age fotostock; 40 inset: justgrimes/Flickr; 40 background: PepitoPhotos/iStockphoto; 41: Harrison Shull/Aurora Photos; 42 top left: Harris & Ewing/Library of Congress; 42 top right: Dennis Cook/AP Images; 42 bottom: Steve Granitz/WireImage/Getty Images; 43 top left: BOB STRONG/AFP/Getty Images; 43 top right: Al Seib/Los Angeles Times/Getty Images; 43 center: Frederick M. Brown/Getty Images; 43 bottom left: Featureflash/Dreamstime; 43 bottom right: WENN .com 6/24/2016/age fotostock; 44 bottom left: Capitolshots Photography; 44 bottom right: Jon C. Hancock/AP Images; 44 top: Harry W. McCormack/Wikimedia; 45 top left: sevenMaps7/Shutterstock; 45 top right: David Bendann/Library of Congress; 45 bottom: Mohammed Anwarul Kabir Choudhury/Dreamstime.

Maps by Map Hero, Inc.

Scholastic Inc., 557 Broadway, New York, NY 10012

SEP   '18

1 2 3 4 5 6 7 8 9 10 R 28 27 26 25 24 23 22 21 20 19

Front cover: Seneca Rocks

Back cover: Glade Creek Grist Mill

Welcome to West Virginia

Find the Truth!

Key Facts

Capital: Charleston

Estimated population as of 2017: 1,815,857

Nickname: Mountain State

Biggest cities: Charleston, Huntington, Morgantown

UNITED STATES
West → Virginia

Everything you are about to read is true **except** for one of the sentences on this page.

Which one is **TRUE**?

T or F West Virginia is the only state to declare independence from another state.

T or F West Virginia produces more coal than any other state.

West Virginia
8WZ 737
Wild, Wonderful

Find the answers in this book.

Contents

THE **BIG** TRUTH!

Brook trout

What Represents West Virginia?

Black bear

White water rafting

3 History

4 Culture

Brad Paisley

This Is West Virginia!

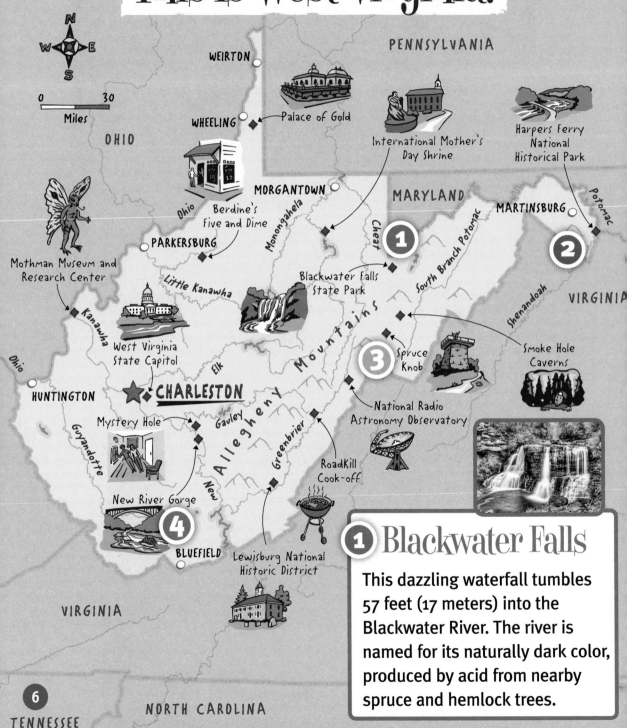

N W E S

0 — 30
Miles

OHIO

PENNSYLVANIA

WEIRTON

WHEELING

Palace of Gold

International Mother's Day Shrine

Harpers Ferry National Historical Park

MORGANTOWN

MARYLAND

MARTINSBURG

Berdine's Five and Dime

Ohio

Monongahela

Cheat

1

2

Potomac

PARKERSBURG

Little Kanawha

Blackwater Falls State Park

South Branch Potomac

VIRGINIA

Shenandoah

Mothman Museum and Research Center

Kanawha

West Virginia State Capitol

Elk

Allegheny Mountains

3 Spruce Knob

Smoke Hole Caverns

★ CHARLESTON

Ohio

HUNTINGTON

Guyandotte

Mystery Hole

Gauley

National Radio Astronomy Observatory

Greenbrier

RoadKill Cook-off

New River Gorge

New

4

BLUEFIELD

Lewisburg National Historic District

VIRGINIA

6

TENNESSEE

NORTH CAROLINA

1 Blackwater Falls

This dazzling waterfall tumbles 57 feet (17 meters) into the Blackwater River. The river is named for its naturally dark color, produced by acid from nearby spruce and hemlock trees.

NEW JERSEY

NEW YORK

② Harpers Ferry National Historical Park

Visitors can tour the fort that John Brown raided in 1859 in a failed attempt to help slaves escape to freedom. The park also contains some of West Virginia's most beautiful hillsides and hiking trails.

ARYLAND

shington, D.C.

③ Spruce Knob

Spruce Knob is the highest point in West Virginia and all of the Allegheny Mountains. It offers breathtaking views of Monongahela National Forest.

④ New River Gorge Bridge

This scenic bridge towers 876 feet (267 m) above the river below. Each year, 100,000 visitors come to celebrate Bridge Day and watch people parachute off the bridge.

ATLANTIC OCEAN

The New River flows through Hawks Nest State Park in southern West Virginia.

CHAPTER 1

Land and Wildlife

West Virginia is nicknamed the Mountain State for good reason. It is the only state located entirely within a mountain range. As a result, it has the highest average elevation of any state east of the Mississippi River. In many ways, West Virginia stands apart from its neighbors. It lies between the northern and southern states. It's also between the eastern states and the Midwest. However, it isn't really part of any of these regions.

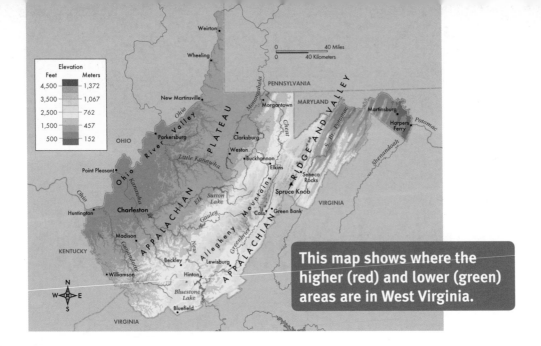

This map shows where the higher (red) and lower (green) areas are in West Virginia.

The Mountain State

About 300 million years ago, two giant **tectonic plates** beneath what is now West Virginia slid toward each other. The land where they met folded and lifted. These folds form a long ridge of mountains called the Appalachians. The peaks of the mountains lie along the east side of West Virginia. The western two-thirds of the state were also pushed up but did not fold into mountains. This region is called the Appalachian **Plateau**.

In the Holler

Between the many mountain ridges of West Virginia are countless valleys. Even the plateau contains thousands of steep, narrow wooded valleys called hollows, or "hollers" by the locals. They were cut from the rock by the movement of rivers and streams. The state's more remote valleys and hollows are sometimes home to families that have lived in the area for hundreds of years. These people tell stories of neighbors and relatives who lived generations ago. For outsiders, visits to these areas can feel like going back in time.

Blackwater Falls State Park contains some of West Virginia's most beautiful mountain views.

MAXIMUM TEMPERATURE
112°F

MINIMUM TEMPERATURE
-37°F

During snowy weather, West Virginia's wilderness often attracts cross-country skiers.

Mountain Weather

What's the weather like in West Virginia? It all depends on the location. The mountains are often colder and wetter than the valleys below. One side of a mountain can also have different weather than the other. The Allegheny Mountains, part of the Appalachians, block clouds floating in from the west. The clouds drop about 60 inches (152 centimeters) of rain and 100 inches (254 cm) of snow each year on the west side of the mountains. The east side of the mountains is much drier.

From the Forest to the Desert

More than three-quarters of West Virginia is covered by forests. In fact, West Virginia is the third most forested state. Monongahela National Forest contains 75 different kinds of trees, including oaks, chestnuts, spruces, firs, and the state tree, the sugar maple. On the state's rainy mountaintops, there are **bogs** and wetlands. Cranberries and wild blueberries grow there. On the dry eastern side of the Alleghenies, however, desert plants such as cacti are more common.

A cyclist enjoys the trails of Monongahela National Forest.

Living off the Land

A huge variety of plants grow in West Virginia's rich forests, and many of them are edible. Some West Virginians go into the forest to pick wild plants to eat. Wild berries and mushrooms are popular and delicious. Ramps, a type of wild onion, are collected throughout the state. Dandelion leaves are used to make tasty salads, and dandelion flowers are turned into wine. Sassafras leaves and roots are used in tea and root beer.

Wild berries are a tasty treat for people, but they are also an important food source for birds and other wild animals.

The People of West Virginia

Elected officials in West Virginia represent a population with a range of interests, lifestyles, and backgrounds.

Ethnicity (2016 estimates)

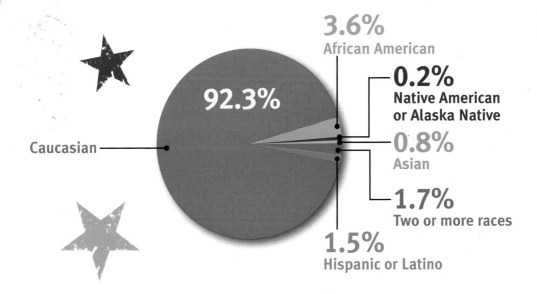

3.6% African American

0.2% Native American or Alaska Native

92.3% Caucasian

0.8% Asian

1.7% Two or more races

1.5% Hispanic or Latino

2% were born in another country.

19% are age 65 or older.

85% graduated from high school.

20% have a bachelor's degree or higher.

2% speak a language other than English at home.

73% own their own homes.

21

What Represents West Virginia?

States choose specific animals, plants, and objects to represent the values and characteristics of the land and its people. Find out why these symbols were chosen to represent West Virginia or discover surprising curiosities about them.

Seal

The state seal features a miner and a farmer standing on either side of a large boulder. The boulder bears the date June 20, 1863, which is when West Virginia became a state. In front of the boulder are two rifles and a liberty cap, symbolizing the state's willingness to fight for freedom.

Flag

The West Virginia state flag includes a wreath of rhododendrons, which are the state flower. It also displays the state motto, "Mountaineers are always free," in Latin.

Brook Trout
STATE FISH
This popular game fish thrives in cool mountain streams like those found in West Virginia.

Rhododendron
STATE FLOWER
This bright flowering shrub grows wild in forests, valleys, and mountainsides throughout the state. Its name means "rose tree."

Bituminous Coal
STATE ROCK
Coal, West Virginia's most valuable natural resource, is found in 43 of the state's 55 counties.

Sugar Maple
STATE TREE
The sweet sap of the sugar maple is used to make maple syrup. It was voted the state tree by schoolchildren in 1949.

Megalonyx jeffersonii
STATE FOSSIL
Fossils of this giant ground sloth discovered in West Virginia were studied by future U.S. president Thomas Jefferson, and the species was named in his honor.

Black Bear
STATE ANIMAL
Black bears can be found throughout West Virginia.

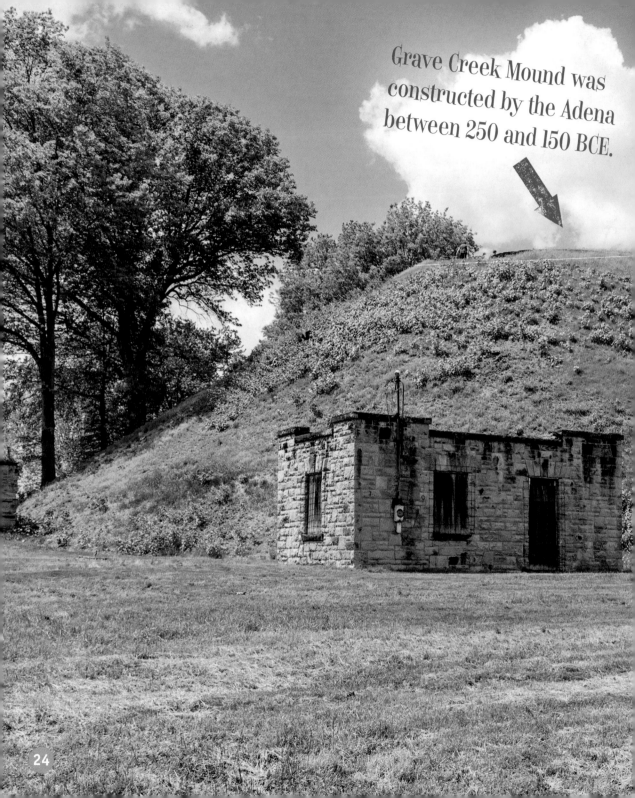

Grave Creek Mound was constructed by the Adena between 250 and 150 BCE.

CHAPTER 3

History

The first humans traveled into what is now West Virginia about 11,500 years ago. They hunted animals and gathered wild plants. People settled down in farms and villages beginning in about 1000 BCE. The Adena people built large, cone-shaped burial mounds made of earth. Many of them still dot the state. The largest, in Moundsville, is 240 feet (73 m) wide and 62 feet (19 m) high.

Early Cultures

Later, other cultures such as the Hopewell people built huge stone mounds. The Mississippian people built big cities and mounds shaped like pyramids. They also farmed crops such as corn. By about 1000 CE, the Fort Ancient culture had emerged. The Fort Ancient people built walled, circular towns with central plazas and houses with straw roofs.

This map shows some of the major tribes that lived in what is now West Virginia before Europeans came.

Native Americans on the Move

In about 1600, the Shawnee, Delaware, and Huron moved into the region. Many of them, in turn, were pushed out by the Iroquois Confederacy, a group of Native Americans from the north whose lands were being

A Huron girls poses for a photo sometime around 1900.

taken by European settlers. When Europeans finally reached what is today West Virginia, many of the first people they met there were Iroquois and Cherokees, who were themselves recent arrivals. After Europeans arrived, things began to change even faster.

Turf War

In the 1600s, England established **colonies** along the Atlantic coast. Settlers from the Virginia colony claimed what is now West Virginia for England. France claimed it, too. Land conflicts between these two countries led to the French and Indian War (1754–1763). Many Native Americans fought for France hoping to save their land from English settlers. England won and forced the Iroquois and Cherokees to allow white settlers into the region.

This map shows routes Europeans took as they explored and settled what is now West Virginia.

Mother Jones

Mary Harris Jones, known as Mother Jones, was one of America's greatest labor leaders. Born in Ireland, she moved to Canada as a teen and later settled in the United States. In her fiery speeches, she urged miners to join **unions** and fight for safer working conditions. During a 1912 **strike** she helped organize in West Virginia, mine owners hired people to beat and shoot union organizers. They had Mother Jones locked up. Unwilling to give up, she soon organized an even bigger strike. In 1921, at the Battle of Blair Mountain, dozens of workers were killed. Thanks in part to the efforts of Mother Jones, workers finally won the legal right to strike in 1935.

Some West Virginians still practice traditional forms of basketmaking.

CHAPTER **4**

Culture

In the old days, the Appalachian region was famous for its homegrown music. Many West Virginians still play fiddles and banjos. The bouncy beat of bluegrass music is great for singing and square dancing.

Popular crafts in West Virginia include wood carving, furniture making, quilting, weaving, and broom making. West Virginia was once a national center of glassblowing, and the art form is still popular there.

Outdoor Action

With no major professional football, baseball, or basketball teams, many sports fans root for the West Virginia University Mountaineers teams. Or they head for the hills and make their own fun. The state's steep slopes attract sledders, skiers, and snowboarders when there is snow. In warm weather, West Virginia's woods are perfect for those who like to hike, hunt, and fish.

The West Virginia University Mountaineers basketball team play home games at the WVU Coliseum in Morgantown.

At the State Fair of West Virginia, young farmers compete to determine who has raised the best livestock.

Fun Festivals

West Virginians love traditional music, storytelling, and crafts. At the West Virginia State Folk Festival in Glenville, there are fiddle and banjo contests, craft workshops, and square dances. Visitors can grab a hot dog or eat something more adventurous, such as frog legs or deep-fried pickles.

Another major event is the State Fair of West Virginia. It is held each August in Fairlea. The fair features rides, tasty food, and more.

Looking Ahead

Glassblowers shape glass objects by blowing air through a tube into hot, soft glass, then allowing the glass to cool and harden.

West Virginia still produces a lot of coal—more than any other state except Wyoming. Oil, natural gas, and chemical factories also supply many jobs. These industries cause a lot of pollution, but West Virginians need the jobs. As mining jobs disappear, however, tourism is growing. Tourists now spend more than $4 billion a year in West Virginia. Many people argue that protecting the state's natural beauty from pollution and destruction is good for business.

Mountaintop Removal

Coal mining has changed since 1990. Most of the state's easy-to-reach coal is gone. Today, instead of digging deep mines, many mining companies use a method called mountaintop removal. They blow a whole mountaintop into rubble to remove a small amount of coal inside. This process leaves behind an ugly landscape. It also causes a great deal of pollution. West Virginians, eager for mining jobs, embraced the new method. But there is little future in it. Once a mountain is gone, so are the jobs.

Mountaintop removal can quickly turn natural forested landscapes into wide areas of barren rock.

Local Treat

Hot dogs in West Virginia come with chili, coleslaw, mustard, and onions—but no ketchup! This combination dates to the 1930s, during the Great Depression. Hot dogs and cabbage were among the few foods widely available, and West Virginians found out they tasted great together. Those who don't like coleslaw can leave out the hot dog and the slaw and make a "chili bun."

Slaw Dog

This West Virginia favorite is easy to make and very tasty!

Ask an adult to help you!

Ingredients
Yellow mustard
1 bag hot dog buns
1 package hot dogs
1 can chili (no beans)
1 carton creamy coleslaw
1 small onion, diced

Directions
Spread a thin layer of mustard on a bun. Add a heated hot dog. Top with the chili, coleslaw, and diced onions. Enjoy!

The Gauley River is a popular site for white water rafting.

Almost Heaven

West Virginia's hills are famous for their beauty. Singer John Denver called them "almost heaven" in his song "Take Me Home, Country Roads." West Virginians loved the song. Many wanted "Almost Heaven" to be the state slogan. In 2006, Governor Joe Manchin proposed a different slogan: "Open for Business." But West Virginians instead chose "Wild, Wonderful." They welcome companies that create jobs. But they also prize their wilderness—and their independence. ★

Famous People

Booker T. Washington

(1856–1915), author of *Up From Slavery*, was born a slave. After being freed at age 9, he moved to West Virginia and worked in a salt factory. He later started Alabama's Tuskegee University to help African Americans become economically self-sufficient.

Robert Byrd

(1917–2010) represented West Virginia in the U.S. Senate from 1959 to 2010, making him the longest-serving senator in U.S. history. He brought many government jobs to West Virginia.

Katherine Johnson

(1918–) was a brilliant mathematician who helped calculate the orbits for the Apollo space program. She was one of the first African Americans to attend West Virginia University and later became one of the first women to author scientific papers for NASA's space program. She was born in White Sulphur Springs.

Betsy Byars

(1928–) is a Newbery Medal–winning author who lived in Morgantown for 20 years. She wrote many books for children set in West Virginia, including *After the Goat Man* and *The Summer of the Swans*.

John Forbes Nash, Jr.

(1928–2015), who was born and raised in Bluefield, won the Nobel Prize for his work in mathematics. His ideas led to major advances in economics and game theory. His life and work became the subject of the movie *A Beautiful Mind*.

Jerry West

(1938–) was a star basketball player for the Los Angeles Lakers. He led the West Virginia Mountaineers to the NCAA finals. His image is featured in the NBA logo. He was born in Chelyan.

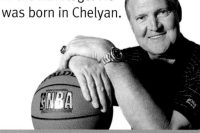

Henry Louis Gates, Jr.

(1950–) is a famous critic and historian. He chairs the African American studies program at Harvard University in Massachusetts. He was born in Keyser, and his book *Colored People* describes his childhood in West Virginia.

Brad Paisley

(1972–) is one of country music's greatest stars, with more than 30 top-ten singles. His grandfather taught him to play guitar at age 8, and by age 10 he was performing in his local church. He was born in Glen Dale.

Cynthia Rylant ★

(1954–) has written more than 100 books for children, including winners of the Newbery Award and Caldecott Honors. Many of her books describe growing up in the Appalachian Mountains of West Virginia. She was born in Hopewell.

Jennifer Garner ★

(1972–) is a movie and television actor who won Golden Globe and Emmy Awards for her role as a CIA agent on the television series *Alias*. She grew up in Charleston, where she performed in musicals at the local community theater.

Did You Know That ...

The Coal House, in White Sulphur Springs, is the only home in the world made entirely of coal.

West Virginia's original capital was Wheeling, but in 1870 it moved to Charleston. In 1875, it moved back to Wheeling—and then moved back to Charleston in 1885, where it has remained ever since.

Organ Cave, in Greenbrier County, is one of the country's largest cave systems. It has more than 45 miles (72 kilometers) of mapped passages, with 200 more passageways yet unmapped.

Many small villages in West Virginia have quaint, old-fashioned names such as Bergoo, Cucumber, Droop, Duck, Left Hand, Mud, Pie, Pinch, Quick, Tad, Tornado, Twilight, and Looneyville.

Thomas "Stonewall" Jackson, born near Clarksburg, was a leading general in the Confederate army, which fought the Union during the Civil War. Many members of his family were staunch Union supporters. His sister Laura reportedly said that she "would rather know that he was dead than to have him a leader in the rebel army."

Did you find the truth? ★

T West Virginia is the only state to declare independence from another state.

F West Virginia produces more coal than any other state.

Resources

Books

Heinrichs, Ann. *West Virginia*. New York: Children's Press, 2015.

Rozett, Louise (ed.). *Fast Facts About the 50 States: Plus Puerto Rico and Washington, D.C.* New York: Children's Press, 2010.

Rylant, Cynthia. *When I Was Young in the Mountains*. New York: Puffin Books, 1993.

Yomtov, Nel. *John Brown: Defending the Innocent or Plotting Terror?* Mankato, MN: Capstone Press, 2013.

Visit this Scholastic website for more information on West Virginia:
★ www.factsfornow.scholastic.com
Enter the keywords **West Virginia**

Important Words

abolitionists (ab-uh-LISH-uh-nists) people who worked to end slavery before the Civil War

bogs (BAHGZ) areas of soft, wet land

colonies (KAH-luh-neez) territories that have been settled by people from another country and are controlled by that country

Great Depression (GRAYT dih-PRESH-uhn) a severe worldwide economic downturn that took place in the 1930s

immigrants (IM-ih-gruhnts) people who move from one country to another and settle there

plateau (plah-TOH) an area of level ground that is higher than the surrounding area

seceded (si-SEE-did) formally withdrew from a group or organization, often to form another organization

strike (STRIKE) a situation in which workers refuse to work until their demands are met

tectonic plates (tek-TAH-nik PLAYTS) large pieces of the earth's outer layer that are slowly moving

unions (YOON-yuhnz) organized groups of workers set up to help improve such things as working conditions, wages, and health benefits

Index

Page numbers in **bold** indicate illustrations.

About the Author

Martin Schwabacher is the author of more than two dozen books for children, including *Minnesota* in the My United States series. He lives in New York City, where he works as an exhibition writer at the American Museum of Natural History.